D1524158

Tools

Search
Notes

Discuss

MyReportLinks.com Books

Go!

STATES

GEORGIA

A MyReportLinks.com Book

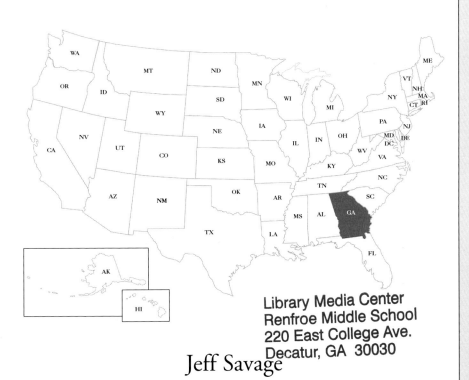

Jeff Savage

MyReportLinks.com Books

an imprint of

 Enslow Publishers, Inc.

Box 398, 40 Industrial Road
Berkeley Heights, NJ 07922
USA

MyReportLinks.com Books, an imprint of Enslow Publishers, Inc. MyReportLinks is a trademark of Enslow Publishers, Inc.

Library of Congress Cataloging-in-Publication Data

Savage, Jeff, 1961–
  Georgia / Jeff Savage.
    p. cm. — (States)
Summary: Discusses the land and climate, economy, government, and history of the state of Georgia. Includes Internet links to Web sites.
Includes bibliographical references and index.
  ISBN 0-7660-5114-5
  1. Georgia—Juvenile literature. [1. Georgia.] I. Title. II. States
(Series : Berkeley Heights, N.J.)
  F286.3.S28 2003
  975.8—dc21
                            2003004156

Printed in the United States of America

10 9 8 7 6 5 4 3 2 1

To Our Readers:
Through the purchase of this book, you and your library gain access to the Report Links that specifically back up this book.
The Publisher will provide access to the Report Links that back up this book and will keep these Report Links up to date on **www.myreportlinks.com** for three years from the book's first publication date.
We have done our best to make sure all Internet addresses in this book were active and appropriate when we went to press. However, the author and the Publisher have no control over, and assume no liability for, the material available on those Internet sites or on other Web sites they may link to.
The usage of the MyReportLinks.com Books Web site is subject to the terms and conditions stated on the Usage Policy Statement on **www.myreportlinks.com**.
A password may be required to access the Report Links that back up this book. The password is found on the bottom of page 4 of this book.
Any comments or suggestions can be sent by e-mail to comments@myreportlinks.com or to the address on the back cover.

Photo Credits: © 1998 Corbis Corporation, p. 11; © Corel Corporation, p. 3; Carl Vinson Institute of Government, the University of Georgia, pp. 37, 42; Enslow Publishers, Inc., pp. 1, 10, 18; Georgia Cotton Commission, p. 12; Georgia Department of Industry, Trade, and Tourism, pp. 15, 20, 22, 23, 24, 26, 31, 32, 33, 35; Georgia Women of Achievement, p. 14; Library of Congress, pp. 28, 29; MyReportLinks.com Books, p. 4; National Archives and Records Administration, p. 16; National Park Service, p. 44; Netstate, p. 10 (flag); Trail of Tears National Historic Site, p. 41.

Cover Photo: Georgia Department of Industry, Trade & Tourism.

Cover Description: Savannah, Georgia.

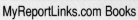
Contents

MyReportLinks.com Books
Great Books, Great Links, Great for Research!

MyReportLinks.com Books present the information you need to learn about your report subject. In addition, they show you where to go on the Internet for more information. The pre-evaluated Report Links that back up this book are kept up to date on **www.myreportlinks.com**. With the purchase of a MyReportLinks.com Books title, you and your library gain access to the Report Links that specifically back up that book. The Report Links save hours of research time and link to dozens—even hundreds—of Web sites, source documents, and photos related to your report topic.

Please see "To Our Readers" on the Copyright page for important information about this book, the MyReportLinks.com Books Web site, and the Report Links that back up this book.

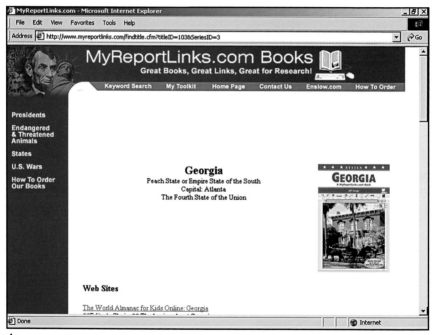

Access:

The Publisher will provide access to the Report Links that back up this book and will try to keep these Report Links up to date on our Web site for three years from the book's first publication date. Please enter **SGA2357** if asked for a password.

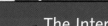
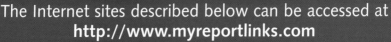
The Internet sites described below can be accessed at
http://www.myreportlinks.com

*EDITOR'S CHOICE

▶**The *World Almanac for Kids Online:* Georgia**
This site contains some basic facts about Georgia. Here you will find
information about land and resources, population, education and
cultural activity, government and politics, economy, and history.

Link to this Internet site from http://www.myreportlinks.com

*EDITOR'S CHOICE

▶**Secretary of State Cathy Cox: Education Corner**
This site from Georgia's secretary of state contains a variety of
information about Georgia. Facts about state history, government,
symbols, and cities are included. A virtual tour of the state capitol
is also offered.

Link to this Internet site from http://www.myreportlinks.com

*EDITOR'S CHOICE

▶**U.S. Census Bureau: State and County
Quick Facts: Georgia**
This site from the United States Census Bureau contains facts and
figures about Georgia. Here you will find population, demographic,
and housing information; economic statistics; and more.

Link to this Internet site from http://www.myreportlinks.com

*EDITOR'S CHOICE

▶**Jimmy Carter Library & Museum**
The Jimmy Carter Library and Museum Web site contains
photographs, information, and documents related to Carter's
presidency. Here you will find digitized documents about the
Iranian hostage crisis and the Camp David Accords, among others.

Link to this Internet site from http://www.myreportlinks.com

*EDITOR'S CHOICE

▶**Explore the States: Georgia**
America's Story, a Library of Congress Web site, contains a number
of short articles about Georgia. Topics include the burning of Atlanta
during the Civil War, the founder of the Girl Scouts, Prater's Mill,
and more.

Link to this Internet site from http://www.myreportlinks.com

*EDITOR'S CHOICE

▶**Georgia Cotton Commission**
Cotton production is important to Georgia's economy, as it has been
throughout the state's history. The Georgia Cotton Commission's site
contains facts, statistics, news, and other information about the state's
cotton industry.

Link to this Internet site from http://www.myreportlinks.com

Report Links

> The Internet sites described below can be accessed at
> **http://www.myreportlinks.com**

▶ **Atlanta Braves: The Official Site**
On this site you can read about the Atlanta Braves, one of the most successful Major League Baseball teams over the past two decades.

Link to this Internet site from http://www.myreportlinks.com

▶ **Atlanta 1996: Games of the XXVI Olympiad**
This site from the International Olympic Committee provides an overview of the 1996 Summer Olympic Games, which were held in Atlanta, Georgia. Images and results of the events are included.

Link to this Internet site from http://www.myreportlinks.com

▶ **Carl Vinson: A Legend in His Own Time**
Carl Vinson spent more than fifty years in the House of Representatives. Here you will find biographical information and photographs illustrating his life and work. Links to the USS *Carl Vinson* can be found at the bottom of the page.

Link to this Internet site from http://www.myreportlinks.com

▶ **The Cherokee Nation: Cherokee Nation Cultural Site**
Members of the Cherokee Nation were inhabitants of northern Georgia when the first Europeans arrived. As white settlement increased, the Cherokee were forced from the state. Here you will find a wealth of information about tribal culture, history, literature, and language.

Link to this Internet site from http://www.myreportlinks.com

▶ **The Civil War in Georgia**
This site from the Carl Vinson Institute of Government contains a wealth of information about the Civil War in Georgia. Here you will find maps, memoirs, battle accounts, photographs, and other resources.

Link to this Internet site from http://www.myreportlinks.com

▶ **Dr. John S. Pemberton (inventor of Coca-Cola)**
This Library of Congress American Memory page contains the biography of Coca-Cola inventor Dr. John S. Pemberton. A brief history of the company can also be found here. Follow the link at the bottom of the page to enter American Memory's Coca-Cola Television Advertising exhibit.

Link to this Internet site from http://www.myreportlinks.com

Report Links

 The Internet sites described below can be accessed at
http://www.myreportlinks.com

▶ **Eli Whitney**
Eli Whitney was the inventor of the cotton gin. His creation helped
jump-start the industrial revolution and the rise of the cotton industry
in America. Here you will read about Whitney, the state of the cotton
industry before his invention, the cotton gin, and the machine's legacy.

Link to this Internet site from http://www.myreportlinks.com

▶ **50 States: Georgia**
At this site, you can find information ranging from when Georgia
became a state to the name of the state song. Be sure to check out
"Fast Facts" for some interesting trivia.

Link to this Internet site from http://www.myreportlinks.com

▶ **The Founding Fathers: Georgia**
Abraham Baldwin, William Few, William Houston, and William Leigh
Pierce were representatives to the United States Continental Congress
from Georgia. This National Archives and Records Administration site
contains their biographies.

Link to this Internet site from http://www.myreportlinks.com

▶ **Georgia.gov**
Georgia.gov is the official site of the state of Georgia. Here you will
find information about the executive, legislative, and judicial branches
of Georgia's government. State news and tourist facts are also included.

Link to this Internet site from http://www.myreportlinks.com

▶ **Georgia Women of Achievement: Honorees**
Georgia Women of Achievement is dedicated to creating a broader
awareness of the important role of women in the history of Georgia.
At the group's site are biographies of notable women from Georgia.

Link to this Internet site from http://www.myreportlinks.com

▶ **Governor Sonny Perdue**
On this site you can learn about the current governor of Georgia,
Sonny Perdue. A biography and images are included.

Link to this Internet site from http://www.myreportlinks.com

Report Links

▶ **James Earl Carter**

This comprehensive biography of Jimmy Carter provides basic facts about Carter in addition to a detailed profile about his life before, during, and after his presidency.

Link to this Internet site from http://www.myreportlinks.com

▶ **James Edward Oglethorpe**

James Edward Oglethorpe was the founder of the British colony of Georgia. This site from the University of Georgia's Carl Vinson Institute of Government contains lectures, images, maps, links, and other items related to Oglethorpe.

Link to this Internet site from http://www.myreportlinks.com

▶ **Juliette Gordon Low, Founder of the Girl Scouts of the USA**

Juliette Gordon Low, a native of Savannah, Georgia, founded the Girl Scouts of America in 1912. Here you will find out about her life and work. Notable facts and an interactive photograph help tell her story.

Link to this Internet site from http://www.myreportlinks.com

▶ **Margaret Mitchell House and Museum: Margaret Mitchell**

Margaret Mitchell wrote one of the best-selling books in the history of publishing, *Gone With the Wind*. Here you will find her biography and time line. Use the links at the bottom to navigate the Margaret Mitchell House and Museum site.

Link to this Internet site from http://www.myreportlinks.com

▶ **The Martin Luther King, Jr., Papers Project**

The Martin Luther King, Jr., Papers Project, from Stanford University's Web site, holds a vast collection of materials related to the civil rights leader. Here you will find audio and text versions of Dr. King's speeches, biographical information, and an interactive time line.

Link to this Internet site from http://www.myreportlinks.com

▶ **Mary Musgrove, Queen of the Creeks**

Mary Musgrove was a Creek Indian in Georgia before it became a colony. Her work as a translator prompted James Oglethorpe to grant her five hundred acres of land. Here you will find her biography.

Link to this Internet site from http://www.myreportlinks.com

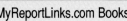
Report Links

 The Internet sites described below can be accessed at
http://www.myreportlinks.com

▶ **National Park Service: Chickamauga & Chattanooga National Military Park**
The Battles of Chickamauga and Chattanooga in 1863 were two of the most pivotal in the Civil War. Here you will find information about the preserved battlefields that became the first National Military Park.
Link to this Internet site from http://www.myreportlinks.com

▶ **National Park Service: Martin Luther King, Jr., National Historic Site**
The Martin Luther King, Jr., National Historic Site consists of the civil rights leader's childhood home and the church in which three generations of Kings preached, Ebenezer Baptist Church.
Link to this Internet site from http://www.myreportlinks.com

▶ **National Park Service: Trail of Tears National Historic Trail**
The National Park Service's Trail of Tears National Historic Trail commemorates the removal of the Cherokee from their homelands in the east, including Georgia, to Indian Territory in Oklahoma.
Link to this Internet site from http://www.myreportlinks.com

▶ **National Wildlife Federation: Okefenokee**
The Okefenokee Swamp is the second-largest freshwater swamp in the United States. This National Wildlife Federation site contains information about the swamp's history, ecosystem, and conservation information. A virtual tour of the swamp can also be found here.
Link to this Internet site from http://www.myreportlinks.com

▶ **Stately Knowledge: Georgia**
This site offers facts about the state of Georgia, including the state's motto, major industries, and geographical boundaries.
Link to this Internet site from http://www.myreportlinks.com

▶ **Supreme Court Watch: Clarence Thomas, Associate Justice**
Clarence Thomas from Pin Point, Georgia, is the second African American to serve as a Supreme Court justice. Here you will learn about his life, career, nomination, and confirmation.
Link to this Internet site from http://www.myreportlinks.com

▶ **Capital**
Atlanta

▶ **Gained Statehood**
January 2, 1788, the fourth
state of the Union.

▶ **Population**
8,186,453*

▶ **Bird**
Brown thrasher

▶ **Tree**
Live oak

▶ **Flower**
Cherokee rose

▶ **Reptile**
Gopher tortoise

▶ **Fish**
Largemouth bass

▶ **Gemstone**
Quartz

▶ **Song**
"Georgia on My Mind"
(lyrics by Stuart Gorrell,
music by Hoagy Carmichael)

▶ **Motto**
"Wisdom, Justice,
and Moderation"

▶ **Nicknames**
Peach State, Empire State of
the South, Goober State

▶ **Flag**
The state flag of Georgia,
adopted May 8, 2003, features
a blue square in the upper left
corner on which the Georgia
coat of arms is printed in gold.
Under the coat of arms are the
words "In God We Trust," and
encircling the coat and words
are thirteen white stars, repre-
senting the thirteen original
colonies. The rest of the flag
features three bands of equal
width but unequal length; the
top and bottom bands are
scarlet, and the middle band
is white.

Population reflects the 2000 census.

The State of Georgia

Georgia is a state with a rich and dramatic history. It was the last and largest of the original thirteen colonies. In fact, it has the largest land area of any state located east of the Mississippi River. Since the Civil War (1861–65), Georgia's population has doubled approximately every fifty years. Its population growth rate is well above the national average. With nearly 9 million residents, Georgia ranks tenth in the country, and it is the third largest of the southern states, behind Texas and Florida. Atlanta, the state capital, is a major center of transportation and

▲ Atlanta, Georgia's capital and largest city, is one of the leading cities in the South.

commerce in the South. About two fifths of the state's people live in the Atlanta metropolitan area. Atlanta is such a progressive city that it was selected to host the Olympic Games in 1996. Because of Georgia's thriving industries, it is known as the Empire State of the South.

▷ The Land of Cotton

For many years, most of the people of Georgia grew cotton for a living. They toiled in vast fields on large tracts of land called plantations. Workers picked the cotton bolls from the stalk and then removed the seeds in a process called ginning. African-American slaves provided the labor for this industry until 1865.

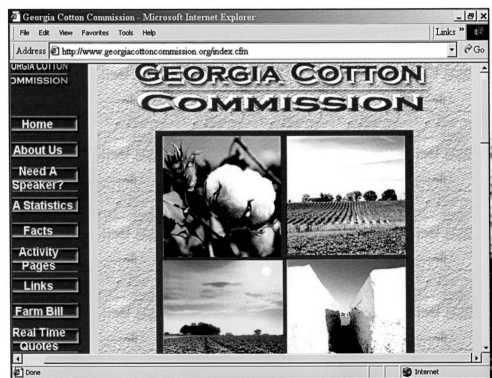

△ Cotton is still "king" in Georgia. In 2002, the state's crops yielded more than 1 million bales of cotton, valued at more than $350 million.

Cotton had many uses. It was sent north to be manufactured into clothes and bedding. Soft cotton balls served as absorbents for doctors and as packing in medicine bottles. African Americans even used a substance found in cotton to treat pain. Cotton has a yellow pigment called gossypol that was said to relieve toothaches and headaches.

The growth of cotton plantations surged early in the 1800s. In 1793, a man named Eli Whitney, recently graduated from Yale University in Connecticut, arrived in Savannah, Georgia, to work as a schoolteacher. Upon seeing the tedious process that workers used to clean cotton bolls, picking out the seeds from the fibers by hand, Whitney designed a simple machine consisting of wires and brushes in a box. Cotton was fed through the machine. A roller turned by hand spun the wires through the brushes. The cotton seeds were separated from the fibers and fell to the bottom of the box. Whitney called his invention the cotton gin, short for "engine."

Cotton became the principal crop not only of Georgia but also of other southern states. It was called "white gold," and the southern states became known as the Cotton Kingdom.[1] In 1791, two years before Whitney arrived in Savannah, Georgians produced about one thousand bales of cotton. Ten years later, in 1801, the state produced at least twenty thousand bales. African-American slaves were shipped to Georgia in record numbers. By 1820, Georgia was the world's largest producer of cotton. By 1860, the state produced seven hundred thousand bales a year.

▶ Four Famous Georgia Women

Many women have helped shape Georgia into a progressive state. Mary Musgrove lived in Georgia before it became a colony. Musgrove knew that in order for the

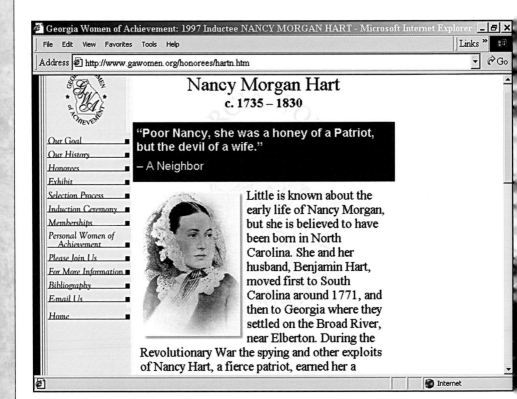

Nancy Morgan Hart
c. 1735 – 1830

"Poor Nancy, she was a honey of a Patriot, but the devil of a wife."

– A Neighbor

Little is known about the early life of Nancy Morgan, but she is believed to have been born in North Carolina. She and her husband, Benjamin Hart, moved first to South Carolina around 1771, and then to Georgia where they settled on the Broad River, near Elberton. During the Revolutionary War the spying and other exploits of Nancy Hart, a fierce patriot, earned her a

▲ Nancy Morgan Hart, who settled near Elberton, Georgia, was an American patriot who spied on the British during the American Revolution. It is also said that she was a sure shot with a musket. Hart County in Georgia is named for her.

colony to survive, English founder James Oglethorpe would need to communicate and establish peace with the American Indians. Musgrove served as translator for Oglethorpe with the Americans Indians. In 1733, Oglethorpe founded Savannah by distributing fifty-acre parcels of land—five acres for a house and garden and forty-five acres for farming—to new arrivals. Women were not permitted to receive these land grants, with one obvious exception: Musgrove was given 500 acres for her vital work as translator.

Nancy Morgan Hart was a doctor who worked as a spy during the American Revolution. She often slipped into enemy British camps to learn what the officers were planning. She was a sure shot with a rifle and was respectfully nicknamed "War Woman" by American Indians. Visitors can see reenactments of her service at Nancy Hart Historical Park, located in Elbert County. Across the county line to the north, Hart County is the only county in Georgia named for a woman.

Other women have contributed to the development of Georgia. Juliette Gordon Low was visiting England when she met Sir Robert Baden-Powell, the founder of the Boy Scouts. Low returned to Georgia, and on March 12, 1912, she founded the Girl Scouts of America. Low's childhood home in Savannah is now the Girl Scout National Center and one of Savannah's National Historic Landmarks.

In 1936, Atlanta author Margaret Mitchell published the novel *Gone With the Wind*, a romantic story of Georgia during the Civil War and the days of Reconstruction. By 1939, more than 2 million copies of the novel had been sold, more than any other book except the Bible, and the story was made into a movie. On December 15, 1939, more than 300,000 people lined Peachtree Street in Atlanta to see actors Clark Gable and Vivien Leigh, the film's leading players, at the movie's premiere.[2]

Margaret Mitchell, the author of the Pulitzer Prize-winning novel Gone With the Wind, *was born in Atlanta in 1900.*

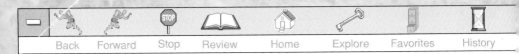

▶ Georgia's Great King

Martin Luther King, Jr., led the civil rights movements of the late 1950s and early 1960s. He was born in 1929 in his parents' home in Atlanta. His father was a minister, and King, Jr., decided at age seventeen to become a minister also. He had entered college two years earlier and was looking for a peaceful means to fight the social evils of segregation. By age twenty-seven, King had earned a doctorate and had become the leading voice in the South against racism. He received as many as forty death threats every day, and once his house was bombed.[3] King never wavered. He led protests and marches in Georgia and Alabama and elsewhere and was jailed several times for "disturbing the peace."[4] In 1963, King led the March on Washington where he gave his most famous speech, known as "I Have a Dream." He proudly attended the signing ceremony of the Civil Rights Act of 1964 at the White House and later that year became the youngest person to be awarded the Nobel Peace Prize. In 1968, King was assassinated while standing on a hotel balcony in Memphis, Tennessee. The house at 501 Auburn Avenue in Atlanta in which King was born and raised was declared a National Historic Site in 1980.[5] In 1986, a national holiday was proclaimed in King's honor.

◀ *Dr. Martin Luther King, Jr., born in Atlanta in 1929, was the leading figure in the civil rights movement in America in the 1950s and 1960s. He is pictured here during the March on Washington, in 1963, which drew more than 200,000 people.*

Land and Climate

Georgia's landscape varies dramatically. From the majestic Blue Ridge Mountains in the north to the many natural harbors along the Atlantic coastline in the south, Georgia is a land of natural beauty. Georgia is bordered by five states and an ocean. To the north are Tennessee and North Carolina. To the west is Alabama. To the east is South Carolina. To the south is Florida. The Atlantic Ocean extends 100 miles along southeastern Georgia. There are so many bays, river inlets, and small islands along this stretch of land that the state has 2,344 miles of coastline.

▶ Six Main Regions

Georgia can be divided into six main land regions. Three of the regions are included in the rugged terrain of the Appalachian Mountain range. They are the Appalachian Plateau in the northwest corner, the Appalachian Ridge and Valley region to the south, and the Blue Ridge in the northeast corner. The highest point in Georgia is Mount Enotah at 4,784 feet, located in the Blue Ridge region. It is also known as Brasstown Bald, because its treeless peak rises above a forest of hardwoods and pines. The Appalachian Plateau ranges from 1,800 to 2,000 feet above sea level, and its thin, sandy soil is not suitable for farming. A better farming area lies in the Appalachian Ridge and Valley, where fertile valleys extend between ridges of sandstone. Fruits, nuts, vegetables, and cotton are grown here, and the grasses are suitable for cattle grazing.

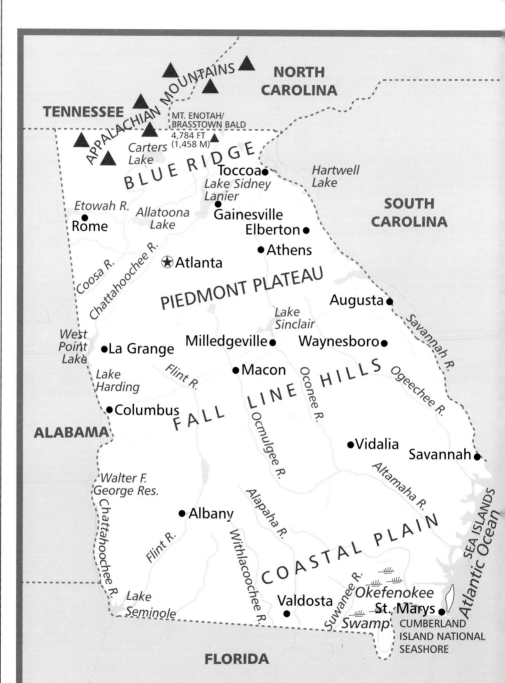

NORTH CAROLINA

TENNESSEE

APPALACHIAN MOUNTAINS

MT. ENOTAH/
BRASSTOWN BALD
4,784 FT
(1,458 M)

Carters
Lake

BLUE RIDGE

Toccoa

Hartwell
Lake

SOUTH
CAROLINA

Etowah R.

Allatoona
Lake

Lake Sidney
Lanier

Rome

Gainesville

Coosa R.

Chattahoochee R.

Elberton

Athens

★Atlanta

PIEDMONT PLATEAU

Augusta

Savannah R.

West
Point
Lake

La Grange

Lake
Sinclair

Milledgeville

Waynesboro

Lake
Harding

Flint R.

Macon

Oconee R.

Ogeechee R.

FALL LINE HILLS

Columbus

ALABAMA

Ocmulgee R.

Vidalia

Savannah

Walter F.
George Res.

Altamaha R.

Albany

Alapaha R.

COASTAL PLAIN

SEA ISLANDS

Chattahoochee R.

Flint R.

Withlacoochee R.

Suwanee R.

Okefenokee

Valdosta

St. Marys

Atlantic Ocean

Lake
Seminole

Swamp

CUMBERLAND
ISLAND NATIONAL
SEASHORE

FLORIDA

▲ A map of Georgia.

The other three regions are the Piedmont Plateau, the East Gulf Coastal Plain, and the Atlantic Coastal Plain. The Piedmont begins at the foot of the Appalachian Mountains and sweeps southward to the area where it meets the coastal plains. The Piedmont comprises 30 percent of Georgia and is the most developed and populated part of the state. The large cities of Atlanta and Athens lie in its gently rolling hills, while Columbus, Augusta, and Macon are situated at its southern boundary. The iron-rich red soil is ideal for farming. The East Gulf Coastal Plain in the southwest is a flatland of rich soil ideal for growing crops. The Atlantic Coastal Plain is similar in appearance and is also well suited for agriculture.

▷ Water, Water Everywhere

Georgia is laced with rivers and dotted with lakes. Among the largest rivers, the Savannah and Altamaha run from the higher elevations of the Appalachians down to the Atlantic Ocean, while the Chattahoochee and Flint flow to the Gulf of Mexico. Dams built on these and other rivers produce most of the state's hydroelectric power. Two dams built on the Chattahoochee River have created Lake Seminole and Lake Sidney Lanier, where trout, catfish, black bass, and pike abound, among other species of fish. Other artificial lakes include Hartwell Lake on the Savannah River, Allatoona Lake on the Etowah, Lake Sinclair and Lake Oconee on the Oconee, and Carters Lake on the Coosa. Carters Lake is the deepest lake east of the Mississippi River.

Okefenokee Swamp is situated in the southeastern corner of the state and stretches into Florida. It is the second-largest freshwater swamp in the United States. The swamp water is dark and teeming with fish and plant life.

Georgia's best-known river, the Suwannee, which was made famous in a song by Stephen Foster, runs through the swamp. Most of the 684-square-mile swamp is protected as a National Wildlife Refuge. The Floridan Aquifer, located west of the swamp, is among the nation's largest underground water supplies. Millions of gallons of water are pumped each year from this aquifer, which is replenished with rainwater.

Plants and Animals

Much of Georgia remains undeveloped. Nearly two thirds of the state is covered by forest. More than 23 million acres across the state are forested. The Chattahoochee–Oconee National Forests combined cover almost one million acres. Pine trees mix with hardwoods in the north and live oaks in

The Okefenokee Swamp, in southeastern Georgia and northern Florida, covers 438,000 acres. Its name, which translates as "Land of the Trembling Earth," comes from the Seminole language.

the south. The vibrant colors of the flowering magnolia, elderberry, and dogwood trees emerge in the spring, when the fragrance of plants and flowers fill the air. Laurels and rhododendrons thrive on the mountainsides in the north, while honeysuckles, daisies, violets, and Cherokee roses spread across the coastal region. Nature enthusiasts count thirty-six hundred plant species in the state, including fourteen hundred species of flowers and shrubs. Swaying in the breeze with the flowery shrubs are such grasses as sea oats, wire grass, and marshland cordgrass.

Georgia teems with animal life. An estimated 100,000 white-tailed deer graze among the grasses. Other animals include bears, beavers, wild boars, foxes, muskrats, opossums, otters, rabbits, raccoons, squirrels, and wildcats. Rivers and swamps are home to alligators, salamanders, frogs, and many types of snakes—some of them poisonous, such as the coral snake, diamondback rattlesnake, and water moccasin. Among the fish that inhabit the rivers and lakes are black bass, bream, catfish, mackerel, pike, rainbow trout, shad, and sunfish.

▷ Conservation Efforts

Georgians take pride in their land and protect much of it through government efforts. The state's tidal marshlands are safe from development, and several forests are preserved as wildlife refuges. The habitats of endangered animals are being guarded so that these species can survive. Several refuges on the islands along the Atlantic coast protect wild horses. Other endangered animals include right and humpback whales, sea turtles, and manatees living in coastal waters, several types of woodpeckers nesting in mountain ranges, and a variety of species of bats. The Nature Conservancy protects other lands such as the

Georgia's longleaf pine-grassland ecosystem, which was once the most prevalent type of plant life in the southeastern Coastal Plain, is dependent upon fire to renew itself.

Moody Forest, which features trees over six hundred years old, and Broxton Rocks, in which more than five hundred species of plants native to Georgia are protected in nearly four thousand acres of rugged sandstone.[1]

▶ Climate

Georgia enjoys relatively mild weather much of the year but is sometimes beset by tornadoes, floods, and severe storms. Its average yearly temperature is 65°F. The state is known for its warm, humid summers and cool, mild winters. Its coldest weather occurs mainly in the mountainous north, especially in the Blue Ridge region, where the average temperature in January is 45°F. The temperature averages 53°F along the coast during this wintertime period. In July, the hottest month, the temperature averages 78°F in the mountains and 81°F on the coast. Georgia averages 50 inches of rainfall per year, with more than 75 inches in the northeast and less than 45 inches in the central part of the state. The mountains are dusted with one or two inches of snow each winter. The most rain falls in July and August, and it is driest in October and November.

Floods, hurricanes, tornadoes, and other natural disasters occasionally sweep through the state. Tornadoes can generate winds of more than 200 miles per hour. In 1903, a tornado devastated the town of Gainesville, killing 203 people. In 1936, a tornado struck the town again, this time killing 187 people. In 1986, another tornado cut a wide swath through Cobb County, located north of Atlanta.

Floods have also devastated the state, destroying crops and killing people and livestock. In 1994, the Flint River flooded an area the size of New Jersey and Delaware combined, killing thirty-one people.[2] Enormous bursts of rainfall occasionally cause flash floods. Tropical hurricanes pound the state's coast. But most of the time, Georgians enjoy pleasant weather for much of the year.

▲ Wild horses like the one pictured still roam free on Cumberland Island, off the southeastern Georgia coast.

Chapter 3

Economy

Georgia's fertile soils have allowed its inhabitants to grow food and live off the land. The area's early American Indian tribes, the Cherokee and the Creek, grew corn, beans, and squash. These crops were called the Three Sisters. The American Indians also hunted deer and other animals and caught fish. The British colonists who followed did the same.

▶ The "Growth" of the Land

Georgia has grown from the ground up. Through the nineteenth century, agricultural crops were its leading products, and chief among them was cotton. Large cotton farms were called plantations. Just before the Civil War, there were an estimated 31,000 cotton farms. Most were small farms owned and operated by families just trying to make a living. Only a few hundred were larger than one thousand acres, and these used slave labor. With the

◀ *Georgia, known for its peaches, ranks third in the United States in peach production.*

abolition of slavery, many people, including some small landowners, were forced to become sharecroppers. They borrowed money and grew cotton for a share of the profits. But as hard as they worked, their debt would be adjusted in such a way that most were never able to repay their loan.

Disaster struck cotton farms in the 1920s when an insect called the boll weevil invaded Georgia and destroyed 5 million acres of cotton. Crop-dusting airplanes spraying pesticides eventually eliminated the boll weevil, but not before many farmers had switched to growing peanuts, pecans, and peaches.

In 1940, about 1.5 million Georgians lived on farms. By 1960, that number had dropped to 400,000. Today, about 10 percent of Georgia's workers are employed in the agriculture business. Georgia remains the top state in the production of such crops as pecans, lima beans, and pimento peppers. Cotton is still grown, as are wheat, oats, corn, sugar cane, and tobacco. Georgia has so many peach trees, especially in its west central areas, that it is known as the Peach State. The sandy soil of the coastal plain is ideal for growing peanuts, and Georgia leads the nation in the production of this crop. Georgians call peanuts "goobers," and the state is affectionately known as the Goober State.

An Abundance of Trees and Minerals

Forests cover more than 60 percent of Georgia. It is no wonder, then, that the state is the largest producer of lumber east of the Mississippi River. The Georgia-Pacific Group, based in Atlanta, is the largest manufacturer and distributor in the United States of wood products such as lumber, siding, and doors. Pulp mills turn trees into wood

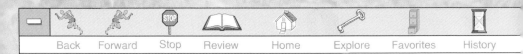

▲ *The state's sandy soil is also well suited for growing peanuts. Georgia leads all states in the production of this crop.*

pulp, which is used to make such paper products as paper towels, bathroom tissue, cardboard, and envelopes. Georgia is America's leading manufacturer of tar and pitch and produces half the world's supply of turpentine, which is used in making disinfectants and insecticides. Georgia-Pacific and other companies replace the trees they harvest for wood. There are more trees planted in the state's rural areas than in any other state in the country.

Georgia is also the nation's leading producer of granite, a hard rock composed of the minerals black mica, feldspar, and quartz. Elberton, located in the northeastern part of Georgia, is called the Granite Capital of the World for its quarries, and the granite mined there is more than 300 million years old. Granite is used to make tombstones, monuments, and buildings. In the early nineteenth century, some of Elberton's granite was shipped north to Washington, D.C., where it was used in the construction of the Capitol building. The Georgia Marble Company, located in Long Swamp Valley, is the world's largest producer of marble. This hard rock is used in many building projects, including some of the nation's most-famous landmarks such as the statue of Abraham Lincoln in the Lincoln Memorial in Washington, D.C. Other mined products include sand, gravel, and kaolin, a clay used in paint and rubber and for coating paper to give it a glossy finish.

Manufactured Goods and Services

Raw materials that are made into finished products are called manufactured goods. Georgia's leading manufactured products are processed foods and beverages, such as peanut butter, baked goods, beer, packaged chickens, candy, and soft drinks. The state's second-leading manufactured goods are textiles, such as carpets and yarn. Dalton, located in the northwest part of Georgia, makes more carpeting than any other city in the United States. Georgia is also among the nation's leading manufacturers of automobiles, aircraft, and missiles.

The best-known company in Georgia is the Coca-Cola Company, which is based in Atlanta. Dr. John S. Pemberton invented the drink in 1886 in a brass kettle behind his house in Marietta, and Coke, as it is also known, became the most popular soft drink in the world. Other large companies with headquarters in the state include Delta Airlines, Lockheed Martin Aeronautical Systems, and United Parcel Service. The Centers for Disease Control and Prevention (CDC) is based in Atlanta. Since 1946, researchers in CDC laboratories have been finding ways to control and prevent diseases. The computer industry is thriving in Georgia

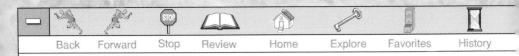
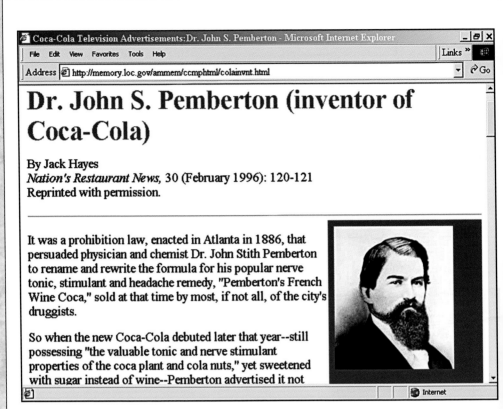

🛑 Coca-Cola Television Advertisements:Dr. John S. Pemberton - Microsoft Internet Explorer   _ 🗗 ✕

File   Edit   View   Favorites   Tools   Help | Links »

Address http://memory.loc.gov/ammem/ccmphtml/colainvnt.html   ▾ ∂ Go

Dr. John S. Pemberton (inventor of Coca-Cola)

By Jack Hayes
Nation's Restaurant News, 30 (February 1996): 120-121
Reprinted with permission.

It was a prohibition law, enacted in Atlanta in 1886, that persuaded physician and chemist Dr. John Stith Pemberton to rename and rewrite the formula for his popular nerve tonic, stimulant and headache remedy, "Pemberton's French Wine Coca," sold at that time by most, if not all, of the city's druggists.

So when the new Coca-Cola debuted later that year--still possessing "the valuable tonic and nerve stimulant properties of the coca plant and cola nuts," yet sweetened with sugar instead of wine--Pemberton advertised it not

🌐 Internet

△ Dr. John Pemberton, the man who "invented" Coca-Cola (better known as Coke), marketed it in 1886 as a "valuable tonic and nerve stimulant." The Coca-Cola Company is based in Atlanta, with more than two hundred offices worldwide.

with such high technology services as hardware and software development and communications services.

Atlanta is the transportation hub of the state and the entire Southeast. There are over 250 airports in the state, and Hartsfield Atlanta International Airport is the largest in size and the second busiest in the United States.[1]

▷ Saying Hello to Tourism

A sign near Valdosta reads: "Georgia is a friend you love saying hello to." With over sixty state parks and historic

areas, Georgia offers tourists many places to see and things to do. In the northern regions, visitors and Georgians alike can pan for gold in Dahlonega, go white-water rafting down the Chattahoochee and Savannah rivers, hike along Georgia's portion of the 2,168-mile-long Appalachian Trail, or visit the Chickamauga-Chattanooga National Military Park, which is the oldest and largest military park in the United States.

▷ O, Atlanta!

In the major metropolitan region of Atlanta, sports fans can enjoy four professional sports teams. The NFL's

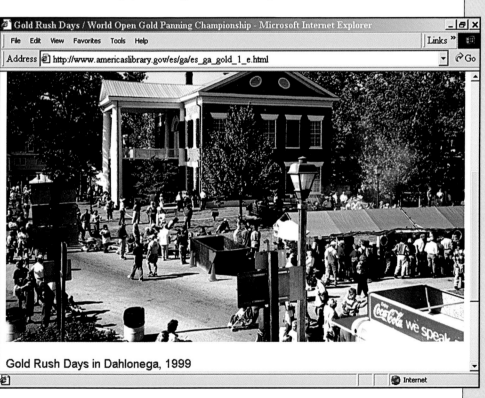

Gold Rush Days in Dahlonega, 1999

▲ The town of Dahlonega, in the foothills of the Blue Ridge Mountains, celebrates its gold-mining past during an annual event called "Gold Rush Days."

Atlanta Falcons play at the Georgia Dome, which was also the site of the 1994 and 2000 Super Bowls. In baseball, the Atlanta Braves play at Turner Field, while the Atlanta Hawks play basketball and the Atlanta Thrashers play hockey at the Atlanta Arena. In 1996, thousands of visitors from around the world poured into Atlanta and nearby towns to attend the Summer Olympic Games.

Many first-time visitors stop along Peachtree Street, made famous by Margaret Mitchell, the author of *Gone With the Wind.* There are no peach trees there, but there are magnolias, camellias, azaleas, and gardenias growing among the white columns of old Victorian houses, where it is said that visiting friends and relatives might stay for a month or a year or a lifetime.[2] Just outside the city is the Stone Mountain monument, which is the world's largest high-relief sculpture carved into the world's largest mass of granite. The likenesses of the Civil War's three greatest Confederate heroes, mounted on horseback—General Robert E. Lee, General Thomas J. "Stonewall" Jackson, and President Jefferson Davis—are engraved in the mountain. The sculpture was started in 1923 by Gutzon Borglum, restarted in 1925 by Augustus Lukeman after Borglum left and went west to carve Mount Rushmore, and completed by Walter Kirtland Hancock of Gloucester, Massachusetts, between 1964 and 1972. The completed sculpture is 90 feet high and 190 feet wide.

▷ The Historic Heartland

To the south of the Atlanta metropolitan area is the region of central Georgia known as the Historic Heartland. In Macon, the region's largest city, visitors can explore the Georgia Music Hall of Fame and the Museum of Arts and Sciences. The 117-mile Antebellum Trail runs from

▲ Visitors to Stone Mountain Park north of Atlanta can take an 800-foot cable-car ride up the mountain for closer views of the Confederate Memorial carving. The carving depicts Robert E. Lee, Stonewall Jackson, and Jefferson Davis.

Macon through Milledgeville, the former state capital, to Athens, home of the University of Georgia. In the town of Perry, which runs along the Peach Blossom Trail, people can pick their own peaches.

▶ The Classic South

The region in east central Georgia is called the Classic South because of its history. Among its oldest towns is Augusta, which was founded in 1735 as a trading post. Visitors can tour the Cotton Exchange Building, where brokers made their fortunes two centuries ago. Every April, the Augusta National Golf Club hosts the Masters golf tournament, which some consider the most prestigious

▲ *The Augusta National Golf Club is home each April to the Masters golf tournament, considered one of the most prestigious events on the PGA tour.*

golf tournament in the world. In nearby Crawfordville, Civil War buffs can explore the Confederate Museum at A. H. Stephens State Historic Park.

▷ The Colonial Coast

The Colonial Coast includes the historic town of Savannah and the thirteen barrier islands known as the Golden Isles, which are part of the Sea Islands chain. Visitors can see more than one thousand historic buildings in Savannah or tour the islands by ferry. To the southwest, visitors can take a guided tour of the mysterious Okefenokee Swamp, with its water lilies, alligators, cypress trees, and flying squirrels.

Government

Georgia's first constitution was adopted in 1777, nearly eleven years before Georgia became a state. In 1788, Georgia officially became the fourth state of the Union when it ratified the Constitution of the United States of America. One year later, Georgia adopted its second state constitution. More state constitutions followed in 1798, 1861, 1865, 1868, 1877, 1945, and 1976. Georgia's current constitution was adopted in 1982.

Georgia's government is similar to the federal government in that power is divided among three branches

▲ *The state capitol, in Atlanta.*

of government: executive, legislative, and judicial. The governor heads the executive branch. The governor is in charge of the budget and other finances. Georgia governors are elected to serve four-year terms and may serve only two consecutive terms. Other elected officials in the executive branch of Georgia's government are the lieutenant governor, attorney general, insurance commissioner, secretary of state, and superintendent of schools.

The legislative branch of Georgia is called the general assembly. It is made up of two "houses." The upper house is called the senate. It has fifty-six senators. The lower house is called the house of representatives. It has 180 representatives. Senators and representatives are responsible for making laws. The state's citizens elect these legislators every two years.

The state's court system is the judicial branch. The courts interpret the law. There are several "levels" of courts, from local juvenile and small-claims courts, to superior courts, to the state supreme court. The highest court in the state, the supreme court, has a chief justice and six associate justices who are elected to six-year terms.

▶ The Capital

Atlanta is the fifth city to serve as the state capital of Georgia. Savannah was the first, followed by Augusta, Louisville, and Milledgeville. But government is not limited to the state capital. There are local government officials and services as well. Of the state's counties, 156 are governed by a board of commissioners. These commissioners mostly are elected officials who serve four-year terms. Some officials are appointed. It is the responsibility of the commissioners, as with all elected officials, to represent the wishes of the people.

▶ A Georgian in the White House

Georgians were rightly proud in 1977 when one of their citizens reached the highest public office in the land. Jimmy Carter served as the thirty-ninth president of the United States from 1977 to 1981. Carter, born in 1924, grew up on a farm in southwest Georgia during the Depression. He helped his family grow crops, and by age five he was selling peanuts on the downtown street corners of Plains, Georgia. He sold each half-pound bag for a nickel.[1] After attending the U.S. Naval Academy and serving in the Navy, Carter joined public service. In 1971, he was elected governor of Georgia. Five years later, he won the presidency. As president, Carter is best remembered

▲ *The president from Plains, Georgia: Jimmy Carter—the thirty-ninth president of the United States and recent Nobel Peace Prize winner— is seen here in the Georgia countryside with his dog.*

for the Camp David Peace Accords in which he helped forge peace between the countries of Israel and Egypt.

Americans have admired Carter for his deep commitment to social justice and human rights. After leaving the White House, he founded the Carter Center, located in Atlanta, an organization that works to promote peace, resolve conflicts, and improve health around the world. Carter is also the most recognized member of Habitat for Humanity, a group that builds affordable housing around the world. "I get a lot more recognition for building houses," Carter said, "than I ever got for the Camp David Accord or anything else I do now since I left the White House."[2] In 2002, Jimmy Carter was awarded the Nobel Peace Prize "for his decades of untiring effort to find peaceful solutions to international conflicts, to advance democracy and human rights, and to promote economic and social development."[3]

▷ Noteworthy Politicians

The Democratic Party controlled Georgia throughout most of its history as a state. Since 1872, Georgians have elected thirty-seven Democratic governors in a row. Two United States senators and thirteen representatives serve Georgia in Washington, D.C. From 1872 to 1964, all were from the Democratic Party.

Several Georgian politicians have attained widespread recognition. In 1883, Carl Vinson was born in Baldwin County. At the age of thirty, Vinson became the youngest member of the U.S. House of Representatives. He was reelected to twenty-six consecutive terms and served more than fifty years in Congress. Vinson fought for a strong national defense. In 1922, Rebecca Felton became the first woman United States senator. Felton was known for

Profile of Carl Vinson - Microsoft Internet Explorer

File   Edit   View   Favorites   Tools   Help   Links »

Address   http://www.cviog.uga.edu/Projects/gainfo/c-vinson.htm   Go

When it came time to launch the carrier, Vinson insisted that his long-time

Done   Internet

▲ *Georgia Democrat Carl Vinson served his constituents for more than fifty years in the U.S. Congress. He was also the first living American to have a U.S. Navy ship named for him when the USS Carl Vinson was dedicated on March 15, 1980.*

advocating women's rights and improving the prison system. In 1973, in Atlanta, Maynard H. Jackson, Jr., became the first African-American mayor of a large southern city. In 1991, Clarence Thomas became the second African American to serve on the United States Supreme Court. Born and raised in Savannah, Thomas graduated from Yale Law School. He was nominated for the highest court in the land by President George H. W. Bush.

History

Georgia was the last of the original thirteen colonies to be settled by Europeans. In 1732, King George II of England granted a charter to James Oglethorpe to settle Georgia. The state is named after this king. However, English colonists were not the first people who lived in Georgia.

▷ The Earliest Inhabitants

Georgia's earliest known inhabitants were nomadic hunters roaming the land about 11,000 years ago. They were descendants of groups who had crossed the Bering Strait from Asia to North America more than 50,000 years ago. These hunters eventually settled in villages, grew crops, and made pottery. About 2,000 years ago, great mounds of dirt were formed into earthworks. The people who designed them are known as the Mound Builders. The earthen mounds, some as high as fifty-six feet, were used as grave sites and ceremonial platforms. Since this period, several American Indian peoples have lived in the region of present-day Georgia, including the Cherokee, Chickasaw, Choctaw, Creek, Gaule, Seminole, and Yamacraw. The two largest groups were the Cherokee and the Creek. The Cherokee, whose name means "cave people," came from the north and lived on the plateaus. The Creek, so named because they lived alongside creeks, came from the southeast and lived on the coastal plains. The Cherokee and Creek hunted deer, caught fish, and grew vegetables. They sometimes bickered over land boundaries, but they generally settled these disputes peacefully.

The First Europeans: The Spanish

The arrival of the first Europeans meant trouble for the American Indians. In 1540, Spanish explorer Hernando de Soto rode through Georgia with six hundred horses and nine hundred soldiers in search of gold. The Indians were friendly to these newcomers at first, but they grew fearful of de Soto's cruel soldiers. Even worse, the explorers brought diseases such as measles and influenza that killed nearly half the American Indian population. De Soto died in 1542, but other Spanish troops built forts, called presidios, on islands off the coast soon after. They fought the French, who wanted a place in the new land. The Spanish eventually fled the islands, leaving behind their forts as well as their farms and horses.

English Settlers Arrive

When England decided to settle Georgia, James Oglethorpe was put in charge of founding the colony. Oglethorpe planned to establish a place where debtors released from England's prisons could start a new life. Other Europeans persecuted for their religious beliefs would be allowed to practice their faiths in freedom in the new colony. It was to be a place, according to Oglethorpe, "to relieve the distressed." Soldiers would defend Georgia and the other colonies against Spanish and French invaders. In 1733, Oglethorpe founded Savannah on the Atlantic coast. Nine years later, his troops defeated a Spanish landing force on St. Simons Island in the Battle of Bloody Marsh. This ended the threat of the Spanish. More settlers arrived, and by 1776, there were

about 40,000 colonists in Georgia, nearly half of them African Americans.

Georgia and the American Revolution

The British colonists living in Georgia had become frustrated with Great Britain and the taxes imposed by the British government. Like other colonists to the north, they were tired of British rule. The Revolutionary War began in 1775 and eventually reached Georgia. The first battle in Georgia occurred in March 1776, when a British warship seized several rice boats in Savannah Harbor. The patriots managed to hold Georgia until 1778, when the British captured Savannah. Within a year, the British controlled nearly all of Georgia. Even after the British surrender at Yorktown, Virginia, in 1781, Georgia was not free. The patriots managed to regain control in July 1782, when troops led by General "Mad" Anthony Wayne drove British forces away. Nearly half the private property in Georgia was destroyed during the war. In 1787, Abraham Baldwin and William Few represented Georgia in Philadelphia and signed the Constitution of the United States of America. Georgia became the fourth state in the Union to ratify the Constitution.

The Cherokee Nation vs. Georgia

After ridding the land of British soldiers, Georgians did the same to the American Indians. In 1817, the government forced some of the Cherokee to move to Arkansas. In 1825, these Cherokee were moved farther west to Indian Territory, which later became Oklahoma. In 1838, after the passage of the Indian Removal Act in 1830, federal troops forced the remaining Cherokee to move to the Indian Territory also. The journey took 116 days and

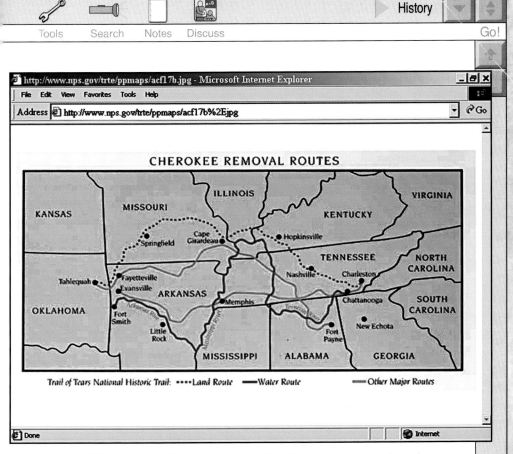

http://www.nps.gov/trte/ppmaps/acf17b.jpg - Microsoft Internet Explorer

File   Edit   View   Favorites   Tools   Help

Address http://www.nps.gov/trte/ppmaps/acf17b%2Ejpg   Go

CHEROKEE REMOVAL ROUTES

Trail of Tears National Historic Trail: ••••Land Route   ——Water Route   ——Other Major Routes

Done   Internet

This map traces the routes over which the Cherokee were forced to travel when they were removed from their eastern homelands, including Georgia.

stretched over one thousand miles. Nearly one fourth of the more than fifteen thousand Cherokee who made the trek in the winter months died from exposure, hunger, or exhaustion along the way. The route became known as the Trail of Tears.

Secession and War

Georgia's triumphs were temporarily halted by the devastating effects of the American Civil War (1861–65). Georgia's economy relied on raising cotton, and slaves were used for much of the work. In 1860, there were

nearly half a million slaves in Georgia. Slavery had existed in Northern states prior to the Revolution, but many Northerners believed that slavery was wrong and had to end. The Southern states believed that slavery was necessary for many reasons.

On January 19, 1861, Georgia voted to secede (withdraw) from the Union. It joined other Southern states to form the Confederate States of America. The Civil War began in 1861. In September 1863, Confederate forces won the first big battle in Georgia at Chickamauga Creek. But the following year, in September, Union general William Tecumseh Sherman's army took Atlanta and, in November, burned much of it. Of the four thousand

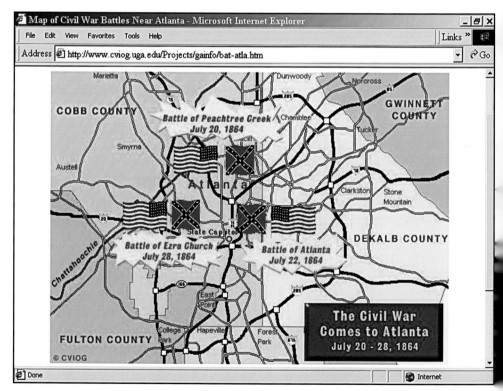

▲ The Civil War battles that took place in and around Atlanta are shown on this map.

buildings in the city at the time, only four hundred were left standing.

Then the Union army devastated the countryside in the course of Sherman's famous March to the Sea. Union soldiers cut a swath sixty miles wide through Georgia, destroying all public buildings, factories, and railroads in their path. The campaign ended with the fall of Savannah in December. When the Civil War ended, Georgia was in ruins.

Reconciliation and Reconstruction

The period following the Civil War is known as Reconstruction. It took hard work to rebuild the land. Slaves were freed, and labor was hard to find to work the cotton fields. Large plantations were divided into small plots, and farmers were encouraged to grow other crops, such as tobacco, corn, and peaches. Eventually, Atlanta recovered to become the premier city of the postwar South.

The growth of manufacturing and trade marked Georgia's emergence as an industrialized state. Factories were built, often with money from businessmen from northern states. Atlanta's railroad system, which was elaborate even before the war, was rebuilt and expanded. At the turn of the twentieth century, mills for textiles and wood products were established throughout the state. Georgians were at the forefront of a progressive movement called the New South. Progress was slowed with the Great Depression in the 1930s, but only temporarily.

A State of Firsts

The first African-American church in the country was built in Savannah in 1788, the same year that Georgia became a state. (The present church structure was built in 1859.) It was one of many "firsts" for which Georgians

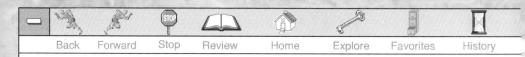
could be proud. In 1819, the steamship *Savannah* became the first steam-powered ship to cross the Atlantic Ocean. It made its successful voyage from Savannah to Liverpool, England. In 1828, the *Cherokee Phoenix* was first printed. This was the first newspaper in America to use an American Indian language. In 1842, a doctor in Georgia used ether in surgery for the first time. Crawford W. Long anesthetized his patient with ether, rendering him unconscious, before removing a tumor from the patient's neck. In 1866, Georgia became the first state in the nation to pass a law allowing women to own property. In 1943, Georgia became the first state to allow eighteen-year-olds to vote.

The Ebenezer Baptist Church on Auburn Avenue in Atlanta was where Dr. Martin Luther King, Jr., was baptized and ordained as a minister; it was also the church where he and his father preached.

▷ The Twentieth Century and Beyond

In the mid-twentieth century, the people of Georgia struggled to overcome the policies of segregation. Such rules required African Americans and Caucasians to use different public facilities, including restaurants, rest rooms, and drinking fountains, and attend different schools. Segregation in public schools was ruled unconstitutional in 1954 by the United States Supreme Court, and in 1960, federal courts ordered Georgia to open all of its schools to all people.

Some residents and business owners resisted the change. They were eventually overcome by those demanding full rights for all citizens, and they were led by a Georgia native: Dr. Martin Luther King, Jr. Protest rallies and marches against racial discrimination were a common scene in the 1960s. The Civil Rights Act of 1964 put an end to the discriminatory practices that had plagued the South since the end of the Civil War. In 1973, Maynard H. Jackson, Jr., was elected mayor of Atlanta. He became the first African-American mayor of a large southern city.

Today, Georgia is a thriving state. Its capital, Atlanta, is a progressive, cosmopolitan city that leads the way in commerce and industry. Yet the easy pace of Georgia of a long-gone era is still found in such places as Savannah. Indeed, Georgia remains a mix of yesterday and today, preserving its proud heritage while moving forward as the Empire State of the South.

Chapter 1. The State of Georgia

1. Gary M. Pomerantz, *Where Peachtree Meets Sweet Auburn* (New York: Simon & Schuster Adult Publishing Group, Inc., 1996), p. 60.

2. Ibid., p. 129.

3. Alex Ayres, ed., *The Wisdom of Martin Luther King, Jr.* (New York: Penguin Books USA, 1993), p. 251.

4. Ibid., p. 256.

5. "Martin Luther King, Jr., National Historic Site," *National Park Service,* n.d., <http://www.nps.gov/malu> (January 29, 2003).

Chapter 2. Land and Climate

1. "Where We Work," *The Nature Conservancy of Georgia,* n.d., <http://nature.org/wherewework/northamerica/states/georgia> (January 30, 2003).

2. "Land and Water Area of States, 2000," n.d., <http://www.infoplease.com/ipa/A0108355.html> (February 4, 2003).

Chapter 3. Economy

1. Gary M. Pomerantz, *Where Peachtree Meets Sweet Auburn* (New York: Simon & Schuster Adult Publishing Group, Inc., 1996), p. 14.

2. Medora Field Perkerson, *White Columns in Georgia* (New York: Crown Publishers, 1952), p. 3.

Chapter 4. Government

1. Jimmy Carter, *Christmas in Plains* (New York: Simon & Schuster, 2001), p. 17.

2. "Jimmy Carter and Habitat," *Habitat for Humanity International,* n.d., <http://www.Habitat.org> (January 21, 2003).

3. The Nobel e-Museum, "The Nobel Peace Prize 2002," n.d., <http://www.nobel.se/peace/laureates/2002/> (February 14, 2003).

Further Reading

Arnold, James R., and Roberta Wiener. *Lost Cause: The End of the Civil War, 1864–1865.* Minneapolis: Lerner Publishing Group, 2002.

Aylesworth, Thomas G., and Virginia L. Aylesworth. *The Southeast: Georgia, Kentucky, Tennessee.* Broomall, Pa.: Chelsea House Publishers, 1995.

Britton, Tamara. *The Georgia Colony.* Edina, Minn.: ABDO Publishing Company, 2001.

Carter, Jimmy. *An Hour Before Daylight: Memories of a Rural Boyhood.* New York: Simon & Schuster Trade, 2001.

Elish, Dan, Kathleen Benson, et al. *The Trail of Tears: The Story of the Cherokee Removal.* Tarrytown, N.Y.: Marshall Cavendish Corporation, 2001.

Girod, Christina M. *The Thirteen Colonies—Georgia.* San Diego: Lucent Books, 2002.

Hutchinson, Duane. *Jimmy Carter's Hometown: People of Plains.* Lincoln, Nebr.: Foundation Books, Inc., 2003.

Kent, Deborah. *Atlanta.* Danbury, Conn.: Scholastic Library Publishing, 2001.

Masters, Nancy R. *Georgia.* Danbury, Conn.: Scholastic Library Publishing, 1999.

Otfinoski, Steve. *Celebrate the States—Georgia.* Tarrytown, N.Y.: Marshall Cavendish Corporation, 2001.

Sherrow, Victoria. *Cherokee Nation v. Georgia.* Springfield, N.J.: Enslow Publishers, Inc., 1997.

Wills, Charles A. *A Historical Album of Georgia.* Brookfield, Conn.: Millbrook Press, 1996.

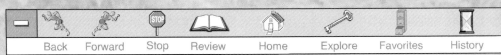
Index

DATE DUE

OCT 0 4 2011			

FOLLETT